I WAS A SCHOOL TEACHER ONCE & OTHER POETICS

Michael H. Brownstein

ISBN: 978-81-19228-84-3

First Edition: 2023
Rs. 200/-

Cyberwit.net
HIG 45 Kaushambi Kunj, Kalindipuram
Allahabad - 211011 (U.P.) India
http://www.cyberwit.net
Tel: +(91) 9415091004
E-mail: info@cyberwit.net

Printed at Vcore.

Dedication: to my beautiful wife, Deborah, children and grandchildren and all of the students I had the opportunity to teach-and who taught me—and, of course, all of the great teachers I met along the way.

ACKNOWLEDGEMENTS

Some of the poems previously appeared in Ten Page Press, Catalysts, The Camel Saloon, A Teacher's Day, Posse Review, Full of Crow, Softblow, Moristotle, Medusa's Kitchen, Cholla Needles Press, and Words, Words, Words.

WHY I TEACH

Introduction:

I never went to war. Korea ended a year before I was born and we lost the war in Viet Nam the year I began college. I never had the hard comfortable friendships true battle inspires and I never had comrades passionate enough to link into that all purpose male code—one man laying his life down for another. No, not me. I never had that.

But fake wars? That's another story. The war on drugs, for instance. I was on the frontlines, a war that threw so much money at itself, it imploded filling prisons and creating cottage industries for curriculum products for every school and community in the nation. It never ends. Just one more victim and one more prisoner and one more person I know who was in the wrong place at the wrong time sending their lives into a spiral downwards so quickly the very system that wants to help ties them into so many knots, it cannot.

I fought in the war against poverty—still do, in fact—and know this war too can never be won. We need poverty for the jobs it gives to us and for the cheap labor and for every gooey Hallmark Christmas story.

There have been other fake wars in my lifetime. Some were firecracker fads, some burnt themselves out under their own weight, and others were so ignored they just vanished and no one remembers.

The good in fake wars is your nightmares are never bloody. You don't wake suddenly in a cold sweat. You never scream out in the middle of the night. At no time do you suddenly slip into a foxhole and find yourself crawling over bodies and pieces of bodies to get away. The participants of fake wars come and go as their interest dictates, not like soldiers who are stationed there waiting for the boredom to become one huge siege of adrenaline and leave with enough material for nightmares for life. No, most fake warriors are never made to stay. Some are in it for a week, some a month, some a year or two. Others make it their life—but they are rare. They become emergency room doctors. Inner city cops. Undercover narcotic operatives.

I became a teacher.

I am not talking about a two-year teacher either—two years in, a best selling book, author signings, TV talk shows. Nor am I talking about teachers who become teachers because this is all they felt they could do. Teaching for a paycheck, in other words. Then there are those who start in the classroom because all they really want is the most direct way to a desk in the board offices. They should have applied there to begin with. Teaching is not about money. It is about passion. I became a teacher because teaching is what I needed to do. The fact that they paid me to do it made it all that much greater. Not too many people can say they get paid for their hobby.

I can.

I can also claim to have had some of the most incredibly satisfying moments in my life teaching school, some of the most inspiring, and there were times I had to walk away so I could shed tears in private. I have lost students to drugs and violence. I have seen students falter to mental illness and devastating sickness. And I have seen students become successful members of the community. One student, for instance, came back to see me ten years after he graduated from my eighth-grade class. "Did you apply for this grant?" he asked handing me a half dozen sheets of paper and I told him I had not. It was just too much work for a thousand dollars. "Mr. Brownstein," he answered, "I'm in charge. Whatever you need, whatever ideas you want to use, let me know. I'll make sure all of them get funded." I wrote the grants over the next few days—ten in all—and he kept his word. The school received ten thousand dollars. We still keep in touch. He has moved up in his foundation, and I am proud of him, but I cannot forget how we talked about him in the teacher's lounge and worried he would not make it past the age of sixteen, his mother a drug addict, his brother a drug addict, his grandmother lost to poverty's skirmishes.

He was one student I reached. There were many more, I am sure, and then there are those I did not. When one of my science fair stars left for high school, she called me monthly for help and I offered it to her. Then she disappeared. I did not know why. A year later she came by the school with her newborn son, but she did not see me. She was too ashamed. I wish I had known this. I would have made her welcome. I would have told her I was still in her corner. I would have pushed her to stay in school and continue towards her goal to be a scientist. That was the last any teacher saw of her, and I did go to her house, but she no longer lived there.

I lost others too, to prison and gangs, alcohol and drugs, victims who could win individual battles, but not the war. Once on the subway I came upon five of my former students robbing a man. They stopped when they saw me, gave him back his possessions at my request and apologized because I asked that of them. It gave me a nice feeling, but it saddened me more—I never went into education to educate children to become lifelong learners of crime.

I have taught in the frontlines for more than thirty-five years. I have published personal views and curriculum ideas and have had articles rejected by editors because they thought they were works of fiction. I taught in the inner city of Chicago. I have never been in a school that did not have less than ninety-six percent of its population eligible for the federal free lunch program. I have taught in schools where I had to check the girl's bathroom to make sure no men were hiding and other schools without bathroom doors so no one could think of hiding.

One time I entered my class to discover a classroom of weapons. Almost every child had something on their desk—a thick stick, a piece of metal, rocks, one kitchen knife. "What's going on?" I asked and they reminded me today was the day a student was transferring into our room from another class, his ten-day suspension over. My class was scared. They knew his reputation. He was dangerous; he hurt people. They reminded me how two weeks earlier he had grabbed some boys and held them hostage in the bathroom. This was before zero tolerance, before every school spent money on security, a time when a touch on a child's shoulder meant good work and it was OK to hug. Somehow I was the teacher who managed to reach out to the suspended student, calm his hostages, calm him, and settle the matter with no one getting hurt. After a few weeks, I knew he really wasn't a bully. He was just a victim in need of nurturing. When we in the school changed the way we dealt with him, he began the slow process of healing. At school's end, he made a few good friends.

There were others like him. Too many to count. There was the girl who was raped by an uncle and withdrew so far into herself, she still has not fully healed. There was the boy who couldn't stand his mother getting beaten all of the time and took his anger out on the younger students. There was the teenager who got a summer job so he could go to college only to have his stepfather steal his earnings to buy whisky. I became a part of these children. I made sure the girl was safe. It took newspaper articles and police, but it was done. I made sure the boy's mother was no longer beaten. I went to his home after school one Thursday and she answered the door with a bleeding lip, a skewed nose, one eye swollen shut. I had come to ask for assistance with her son, but that matter fell to the wayside. "How do you pick a man?" she asked. How did I know the answer? But I knew where she could get help. I knew where she could get counseling. I knew where she could learn how to rebuild her family and her own self-esteem. I was able to offer her that, and I did. By the end of the year, he no longer bullied little children. He became a classroom superstar. And I went into the housing project and into the apartment of the stepfather who had stolen the money for liquor. I asked everyone to leave the room so he and I could talk privately. What was I thinking? He was bigger and he was stronger, but I was right. I told him we would solve the problem now—however he wanted. It did not make a difference to me. He gave the money back and I kept it for the remainder of the summer for safekeeping.

I will not leave my place in the trenches. I will continue to fight the best way I can—thirty-five years and counting—winning battles and losing battles, and I will never go down for lack of trying. I refuse to give up on this war. I figure I have at least twenty more years to give.

A Conversation Between Teachers in the Teacher's Lounge

We wonder what is in the water. Sugar,
Cookies, ripe persimmons, cotton
Candy. We know it is not any of these.
Some things are valued less.
Everything is always that simple.

A Teacher Catches the Elevated to go Home Work

Himidulah and his small friend
Ride the elevated for practice.
"Keep your little friend safe,"
The man reading the poetry journal says.
Himidulah leans inward. "Yes,"
And he adds emphasis to the S
As a sign he understands respect.
"These are fields of poison oak and shrapnel."
The man continues, "Heading downtown?"
"No," Himidulah answers. "My auntie's house,"
And his friend calls to him, the train sways,
A door opens, and they go to the next car.

The man turns the page and leans back.
Once upon a time he met a killer on the train
(Not a killer yet, but one growing inside),
"Should you be with these older boys?"
He asked turning the page of a Kafka short story.
"Yes," the child answered. He too
Knew the respect in the letter S.
"Poison ivy is not a practiced skill,"
The man said. He remembers
How he could not deface the situation,
How he let the child go his way.
They threw the boy into the cold lake
And only luck and thick ice saved him.
Five years later he killed his first man.

Keep the child safe. It is that simple.
You can never practice enough.

And once in the time of rural kings and popsicles,
The man boarded the train and saw two pairs of twins.
"Excuse me, gentleman," he said, "put away
The guns, please, and give the gentleman
His wallet. Apologize. Come sit by me.
I have a need for these guns."
The elevated rolled, but the man stood still
In the aisle and watched. "Deep and unsettling
Is the prairie grass," he said. "Damp and alarming."
He leaned back into the seat and closed his eyes
To everything around him. He slept.

They think we are all made for God,
That some of us do not practice more.
This is the fine tune of the cello.
The man on the elevated listens to the breath
Of the others. There would be other opportunities
To watch the play of little ones,
Find the thought meant to cover everything.
Poison oak, poison ivy, the dark and damp
Tall grasses hiding everything and nothing.
Outside the window thick with grease and air
The sun shines with earnestness bright
And perfect, mounting the sky, letting
Its years of experience shine.

1.

Mary Hilker stands outside her classroom every morning as her students come up the stairs. "Good morning, Billy," she says and then she reaches out and shakes his hand. "Good morning, Angela" and she shakes her hand. Every student, greeted, hand shook, and then she closes the door, watches her students take their seats and she watches as they begin their board work. She does not get wipes for her hand or excuse herself to go to the bathroom. These are her students, her family, and you do not disrespect family. Later she may wash her hands. Before lunch she will definitely wash her hands. But not now. Now she has to teach, and she does, everyday the same routine—this is what I expect from you today, this is how you do it, let's practice, she tells the class.

Mary is a new teacher, fresh out of college, enthusiastic and excited to be teaching. And for some reason she chose to teach in the inner city of Chicago.

Why?

"I came to teach in Chicago," she answers, "because the inequality in schools in America leaves me unsettled and frustrated. However, if I did not take action against that extreme frustration, I felt as if I had no right to complain or be angry. Because the passion to be a teacher and make a difference in my youth was already instilled in me, I decided to make a move to an inner-city atmosphere in which I would do my best to lessen the achievement gap. Chicago was the best option because it was still relatively close to my hometown in Michigan and I felt like it was "on the map" unlike Detroit. I was also very motivated by Jonathan Kozal's "Savage Inequalities."

What lessons have you learned?

"Hard lessons. Are facilities and materials unequal in what I have seen, yes, but so are so so so many other factors. The work ethic and knowledge in the majority of not only the children, but CPS administration, staff, teachers and parents are also huge factors in many of the issues that the students of Chicago face. I want to be clear on that one. I am speaking on basis of majority, there are many exceptions, and as a result of their being so many variables, there is no one quick fix and no one finger to point. With this being said, it is often not just the facilities or the behavior of the children that prevent proper learning from taking place, it is parents and other decisions made by adults. I do not blame these children or these other adults, I blame the lack of knowledge, the lack of opportunity for individuals to "get out" and really know what effective parenting and professionalism truly is. I also place blame on the lack of high standards that not only do some teachers have for their students, but also that the CPS administration has for themselves. There are so many excuses in every direction I began to fall victim to the excuse game—not doing everything that I should have been doing as a highly effective teacher."

During my time working with Mary, she began to further her education by taking algebra classes so she could teach algebra to a select group of upper grade students. She continued with staff development. She assisted me in the after-school program. I recruited her because I knew she would be an asset to the program. But when the program began to fall into disarray for a number of reasons (many within my control and many beyond my control), she told me she did not want to participate anymore, I did not accept her resignation. Instead I asked: "What can I do to keep you?" She told me and I tried my hardest to do as she asked.

We completed the after-school program together.

—-

Tempers are not something easily held. Students know this. They understand how to get a reaction from a teacher and they know how to prolong it.

Not everywhere.

In the inner city, a lack in self-discipline becomes self-evident quickly and the way you as a teacher react to it can change the course of your classroom teaching overtime.

And I won't lie—I was a great yeller. I could out scream, out temper tantrum, out fuss and out—I was very good at it.

But this is not something to brag about. The students who do not have self-discipline quickly learn how to get out of doing schoolwork. The students with learning problems soon figure out how to get out of schoolwork.

I had to change.

It took years—and this is unfortunate because we as teachers see students every year and it doesn't matter if we are a first-year teacher or a tenth year teacher. We do a very bad service to our students when they can manipulate us into a behavior we do not want them to have.

So I changed. One class helped me. We put a large glass jar on the desk and every time I yelled, I had to feed it a quarter. I stopped yelling fairly quickly.

Another class decided schoolwork was not for them—and though every classroom has exceptions and students who really want to learn—this particular class did not. And then I understood. They had failed for the most part at least one grade and they were afraid to fail again. Can't read, disrupt. Can't do math, disrupt. Science became the key. They loved to do hands-on science experiments and we went from simple experiments to full-fledged lab reports—and in here they began to read and they began to do math and the best thing of all was they were doing the very subjects they were most afraid of and becoming good at them.

In the end, I learned to speak softly. To never raise my voice. But it took time. Time is not something we always have.

And my rules worked well, too. So I used them. We discussed them the first day of school and the second and the third and whenever a new student transferred into the class and when it was obvious we needed to take another look at them. They were posted on the front board:

Classroom Rules

No talking without permission.

No touching each other. Touching leads to fighting. No fighting is tolerated at all.

No signifying. No cursing. The "n" word is a curse word. Remember that.

Treat everyone the way you want to be treated.

Follow the rules of the school.

Expectations

If you have a question, ask. You cannot learn if you are afraid to ask questions. There are no stupid questions, just stupid people who did not ask and never found out the answer.

Respect each other. We are the family of Room 112. As a family, we work together, play together, try together and get along together.

Two and three-year olds do not know how to share. This is their developmental stage. We are more mature, able to work out our problems without cursing, fighting or acting ignorant. (Everyone in here knows what ignorant, embarrassing behavior is.)

Everyone has his or her strong points. Few individuals are good in everything. Remember Albert Einstein, the smartest man in the last century, had serious learning disabilities.

There is no I in the word team. Be considerate of your classmates and help them to strive to do better.

Try your best. Give it your all. Be a champion of learning.

Consequences

If you break anyone of the classroom rules three times in one day, Mr. Brownstein will go to your house. (You can get your name off the punishment paper if the class behaves in the hallways and prep classrooms and/or if an adult compliments us anywhere anytime.)

After Mr. Brownstein has made three home visits, he no longer goes to your house. Instead, you will be sent to the office for time-out, parent conferences, and/or suspension.

We will go on a field trip each month. Field trips will be cancelled if anyone in our class has a fight in and around the school and/or one of our students walks out of a class without permission.

Well behaved students or students who are trying extra hard will receive positive home visits or positive home phone calls.

Going to the student's house worked best. And my students knew I would do this. Soon new classrooms of students would not make me lose my temper because new classrooms had already heard—he does go to your house. But not only for bad news. For good news, too. And they knew I only called a student's home for good news. It got to the point parents waited for my weekend call after I had graded everyone's test day paper.

—-

Mary Hilker received the first "You-Can-Teach-Old-Dogs-New-Tricks Award." I gave it to her because of her polite demeanor and how she impacted positively with the student's she taught.

The handshakes when the students entered her room.

Her rules—including one that she held firmly: "No name calling and never tell anyone to shut-up."

And she always tried her best.

2.

There are great periods of distress in the life of a teacher. This distress is not caused by some knowledge leaking away or a student not catching on; this distress is due to constraints placed on the teacher from beyond their control. A problem happens at home and right as the bell rings, something jumps off—an argument, perhaps, or a student so mad he throws an object across the room. We have strategies to deal with these incidents, but we are not always prepared.

Julia was one of these. A highly unpopular girl for no reason at all, she badly wanted to fit in. Most of the time her peers ignored her, and I tried to get them to include her, and I did a lot of character education and leadership work with my class. We were never to be a classroom of bullies—we were always to be a classroom of leaders. Followers have their place, of course, but my classroom is my family—and everyone would always be safe within its confines.

So I worked with Julia and helped her to shape herself. I found many reasons to compliment her and many ways to bring her into the class as a whole. She was not an awkward seventh grader nor was she stubborn or slow to catch on. For some reason, my class did not want to include her. She tried and I tried and then one morning she walked into the classroom with a new look—extensions to her hair, her hair perfectly framing her face, and when she smiled, everything came together.

There was no way my classroom could not take notice of her. And they did. Students complimented her, students made her smile with kind words, students asked if they could comb her hair or simply touch it. We knew her longer hair was due to extensions, and we also knew time and money had gone into this hairstyle and Julia was transformed by it.

What none of us knew was how jealous one of the girls was secretly becoming. She complimented Julia along with the others and talked to her about this and that and I actually believed a breakthrough moment was on hand. An hour later all hell broke loose. This same girl who was quietly working on an assignment three rows and four seats removed from Julia suddenly launched from her seat knocking her desk and her neighbor's desk over falling onto Julia with such a ferocity, I did not know where her anger had come from.

I do not allow fighting anywhere around my class and everyone who knows me knows this. My students either get out of the way or they intercede. This time they did both and by the time I was there, the fight was over, but the damage was done. Two braids were lying on the floor and Julia was in tears.

The other girl was suspended, of course, and Julia's mother came the next day and transferred her daughter out of the school. She, too, had tried to assist her daughter, and the efforts had failed.

The aggressor never said she was sorry to anyone, she never gave a reason why, and her silence and lack of conscience added another day to her suspension.

I can still see the two braids on the floor of my classroom, Julia standing by a knocked over desk, the other girl trying as hard as she could to pull free of the others holding her back—the great anger on her face, her eyes red, her mouth slightly open, her hands clenched in a violence too great to foretell. And I remember my rage—growing in me exponentially until I could not hold it in. I slammed the door to the classroom, felt the glass rattle, sat on the edge of my desk—took a deep breath, asked one of the students to call for security, asked others to help clean up the mess, asked myself to calm down—calm down—calm down, my face so hot sweat trickled into my eyes.

I wanted more than ever to be able to hug Julia at that moment, let her know everything would be OK—but we were not allowed this action—so I sat on the edge of my desk and surveyed the scene, the aggressor no longer in a fighting mood now quietly standing near the door waiting for what would happen to her next.

I had failed—myself, Julia and perhaps most of all, the young lady who missed four days of school.

We never saw Julia again.

3.

Sometimes it's better to just roll over and stay in bed.

A few years ago students from the 8th grade came rushing into my room. "Our teachers fighting!" one of them yelled.

I just knew I misunderstood them. What they must have meant was their teacher was breaking up a fight. But, no. Their teacher was fighting. Three 8th graders were trying to hold him back and a special needs student, about six feet away, was staring him down.

I grabbed the student and pushed him into his classroom. I know I told his teacher to keep him there. Then I rushed back to the teacher in question. He wasn't just angry. His eyes were empty. His fists were clenched hard enough to crack walnuts. He walked towards the special needs student's classroom and even when I touched his shoulder and blocked his way, there was no response. He was past angry.

I turned.

Didn't I tell the special needs teacher to keep her student in the room? Why was he back in the hall?

The teacher roared, tried to get past me, his 8th grade students falling to the side as he let out a steaming bellow of rage. There was only one thing to do. I grabbed the student and literally lifted him to the stairs and down to the first floor where security from the office was now running.

Fast-forward a few years: A student with her mother and aunt entered the playground, scouted the scene, saw their prey and sent the student after it. The next thing I knew, I was in the middle of a fight between two girls—and a mother and an aunt. The first time the aunt pushed me out of the way, I thought it an accident. The second time, I knew it was on purpose. It took three men to break up the fight—and one security guard to get the adults out of the way.

"Let them fight," the mother yelled, and she made room for one of her sons to start kicking. Where is it stated we should allow students to fight?

I'm wondering why the police weren't called.

That was only fight number one.

Life lesson 1: Even though I walk four miles a day to work, I was out of breath. Walking is not enough.

Life lesson 2: Those of you who are pro-life—if you want to end abortions, then start supporting the individuals who have babies with no clue how to parent them. Support them with money and your actual physical attention. Put your money where your idealism is. It's easy to say you're pro-life, but don't just say no to abortion. Say yes to making sure the newborn baby is well taken care of—and I don't mean just through the cute years. I mean through the age of eighteen. Then you can tell me you're pro-life.

4.

Positive Coaching Alliance

Dear Positive Coaching Alliance and " Nike/Go,

Just so you know: I hate professional development. Much of it is just old things with a new name. A lot of it is presented by boring speakers and people who insomniacs should hire so they can get a good night's rest. Even the exciting research we need to know if we are to become better educators is presented in such a way you have to bring personal business with you just to get through the hours and hours of—well, you get the point.

Not so with the Positive Coaching Alliance sponsored by Nike/Go. I was asked to coordinate the After School All Stars and one of the programs I was asked to go to was a Nike/Go professional development. I signed up, but I did not want to go.

Let me tell you—I usually look at the clock every thirty seconds (time moves that slow in professional development land), but I did not turn around once to see the time at the Nike/Go presentation. In fact, when the presenter said it's time and she's sorry she went over by a little bit, I thought: What? Time? No, I need more. I want more.

So I was very excited when I was given the chance to invite the Positive Coaching Alliance to my school. NIKE/GO had given the Chicago Public Schools a grant and I applied and the next thing I knew, we were going to be offered professional development for a segment of our professional community.

OK. OK. So you think all they wanted to talk about was sports and coaching. Sure they did. But that wasn't all. The three individuals who came to my school for the two workshops offered viable alternatives to a lot of the problems any urban school has. Fights on the playground. Cursing in the halls. They gave us actual how-to examples to change the climate of the school. Issues in the lunchroom. Conflict after school. They offered us so much—well, you get the point.

Because of this program, here is how my life as a teacher changed:

My classroom will use the Notre Dame motivational method: I will have a sign affixed permanently to my door. It will say: "Today we will take another risk in learning because we are brilliant." As the children come into the class, they will high five it—just like the college players at Notre Dame.

My classroom letter to all of the parents will also be placed on index cards so when I help in the playground, I can give my expectations to parents who are also on the playground. I will also make sure this card is distributed to adults before all of our sport events. No more crazy soccer mom's for me.

I will use the ELM model: effort, learning and rebounding from mistakes.

I will fill my student's emotional tank.

I will teach my students to honor the classroom and become the best they can be through mastery, risk taking and fair play.

When a child makes a mistake and he/she is embarrassed, I will make the flushing down the toilet gesture to let them know it's OK to make a mistake. We've flushed it down the toilet. Now let's move on. Making mistakes is one of the ways we learn.

I will offer the following criticism when I have to correct misbehavior: "This is not how we do things at this school. How should we correct this problem?"

Thank you.

—-

Carneades of the Word

—And how many men I have seen in my time made stupid by rash avidity for learning! Carneades became so mad about it that he had no time left to take care of his hair and nails.

Michel de Montaigne—

"Of the Education of Children," 1588

Carneades of the shadow.

Carneades of the whisper.

Carneades who could not blink his eyes following letters across a page.

It is good to know prosperity.

It is good to have loyal servants.

Carneades held books close and stubborn

As if his greatest need was to understand the inside of a stone,

The workings of a six-inch tooth washed up on the shore,

The breathing heart of the baby harp seal panting heavily away from others.

Carneades owned all of the books—

Alexander be damned—

His eyes, his ears, his huge sense of smell, unruly hair, broken fingernails—

He read past the moon hour, past the rising of the sun, past the closing of the baths,

Left important matters to his servants

And his servants lived well.

Carneades sits on the soft pillows in the corner of his library,

His lamp bright,

His glasses thick and bulky,

His hair unkempt and ragged,

His fingernails long enough to get in the way of turning a page.

Carneades reads.

5.

Frank Christensen teaches overseas. He once taught in a rough housing project on Chicago's far Southside, so far away, in fact, that many Chicagoans do not even know of its existence. He taught English and because of his passion for English, he taught William Shakespeare. And because of his passion for Shakespeare, he talked the community center director into letting him use the stage a few times a year to let his students perform Shakespeare's plays on the stage to their parents, community members and friends.

So what's the biggest difference between Viet Nam and America?

Frank Christensen tells me there are a lot of differences.

But the biggest one?

Spiritual poverty.

I tell him I met a woman from Ecuador once. Yes, she told me, spiritual poverty. America has big stores and great shopping. That's not enough. There is no spiritual richness in America.

Frank has been in and out of the United State a lot during the last few years. Spiritual poverty, he repeats. That's a problem.

The Woman from Ecuador Speaks

It's not that America is a great country,
I'd just rather be home.
In my country, poverty is very real,
but here there is a greater suffering.
Home, I fill myself with poets,
storytellers, those with idealism.
Home, we give honor to the teacher.
Your country breeds a spiritual anger,
a poverty more devastating
than a lack of food, a lack of clean water.
Why can't Americans wait patiently in line?
Where is it written a house needs a five
car garage? A phone in every room?
A diamond to die for? A video player
to fight over? I would rather own
a gem of verse, a storyteller's laugh line,
knowledge from a teacher.
Those are things to die for. I have to go
home. The water is too shallow here.

6.

I forgot to set the alarm clock, but that's not that big a deal. The sun hit my window at just that correct angle and it made eye contact with my brain. I never stay in bed when I wake. I always get up and do all the things anyone who teaches school has to do—shave, wash up, etc. OK.

So far so good.

The weather report could not have been better. When I walked outside at 5:45 AM, the sun was already rising, the sky was already blue, and I felt good with the world.

I always come to school an hour to an hour and a half before it starts. I like the quiet. I like the peace. I like the solitude.

For the next hour or so, I wrote a poem, revised another, printed some material and prepared my classroom for both reading and science class. During science, we were going to cut open a full-grown pig's stomach. I purchased a few at the butchers and they have been in my freezer waiting for this day. I placed the stomachs on the science table, prepared my desk for the morning's school business, and ate some breakfast. (I never eat at home. I walk four miles to school each morning and it doesn't quite work out if I eat before I walk.)

I went outside to assist on the playground at 8:30. I don't have to go outside, but I do. It was quiet, two men—a teacher's aide and a janitor—were standing near the fence away from the children, a pick-up basketball game was going on, children were all over the playground equipment, but there—over by the wooden playground equipment—something was getting ready to happen.

Sometimes you can just smell it.

I walked over there. One adult was standing behind the equipment, but she could not see this. Two boys, not very big, but big for second and third grade, were getting ready to fight. They made the appropriate motions; their chests and heads played the part of the nonverbal communication. Nothing had to be said. Suddenly students from all over were running because they knew.

I broke it up. It was not hard because even though they were very large for their age (already five feet tall), they were still primary grade students. One of them ran in the other direction. I didn't know who started it and I didn't care—I took the one who has started many playground fights. He was not happy, but I can talk to him. When I told him to smile, he changed from an angry child to an ordinary child. (Why doesn't he smile more often—but then I know too much about his family's background.)

We walked towards the school when the other boy ran up on him, hauled back with all of his might, and it was only because I moved the boy I was restraining to the side, that the punch didn't cause serious damage. I realized immediately that I has to stop this other child—and I did.

I grabbed him by the arm and he fought me. He actually fought me. But that's OK. This is part of my life. This is part of my job. I knew for sure when I had him restrained, he will calm down, probably start to cry, and then we could find out what was really going on.

That did not happen.

He started cursing me and hitting me—one time to the chest, a second time, a third—and he cursed and threatened to bring every one of his relatives on me. He yelled out to everybody on the playground that I'm dead meat. His mama's going to kill me. His father is going to slice me up. He himself is going to knock the color right off my skin. He used the N word twenty times. He threatened and threatened. I didn't hit him back. I didn't say a word. I just held onto his arm and walked him into the school where he continued to yell and threaten and curse and the front office called the police.

Here's the interesting part. When the police arrived, he swung on the woman police officer. She didn't lose it either, but she could take him into a private office and give him a talking to.

I went back to the playground.

It was like nothing has happened.

The boy's grandfather came, I received a police report, and then I went to my class. It was nice in my class. Quiet. My students were ready to study. I felt good. OK, not perfect, but good. One glitch doesn't destroy a day.

An hour and a half later I received a girl from another room because she walked out of her room.

A fight broke out in another class. Both students end up in my room. The teacher down the hall sent a note asking for help. Three students would not stay in the room. The substitute next door complained about students throwing things at her. "Hey," she said, "I'm a sub. I'm supposed to take abuse." I had to get a desk from another room.

Then I had my break. My preparation period. I passed out progress reports. I took the intermediate science genius group from other classrooms and we did a chemistry experiment. The first part worked; the second was a great failure. I passed out field trip permission slips from another teacher when my class came back to me right before dismissal. I had been told by her not to give a slip to one of my girls. I didn't. As soon I dismissed my class, my student was outside cursing the teacher out. I'm sure that changed her mind.

And now the principal wants to meet with me. It's important. Can you come see me before you leave?

I can't leave. I have to vent. I have to get all of this out of my system. I have to—you get the point.

I have to go home because this is a horrible, horrible, terrible day.

—-

The next day: I woke before the alarm clock, was out of the door five minutes early, the weather perfect— perfect sky, perfect breeze, perfect temperature—and one of my former colleagues drove up to me one mile into my walk and offered me door to door service to my school. How cool is that!

I wrote some, revised some, answered correspondence, and prepared my classroom for the lessons of the day. These included a show and tell of African artifacts, some dating back hundreds of years, some recently purchased. I practiced the scary story I was going to tell—a story that actually happened to me many years ago and I prepared for the third day of the scary story/science fiction week. Then I went outside even though I didn't have to and I walked around the playground. Everything was quiet. The too-good-to-be-true kind of quiet. And it stayed quiet. Yeah!

My classroom came in quietly too. I told my class my scary story and asked for persuasive essays on if they thought the story was true or not. I received great responses. Then we read a portion of Ray Bradbury's speculative science fiction—and again the class did great. Great responses. Great discussion. I pulled out my African artifacts and you could hear a pin drop. Another great activity. When we switched classes, the next room did just as well. Whoopee!

After lunch I introduced my room to the first concepts of trigonometry. They paid attention. They took notes. They were engaged. They were excited. I was excited. They were catching on. Super dooper!

Teaching is like this—one-day everything that can go wrong does, but the next day everything that can go right goes right. There's no stopping the momentum of a great day.

7.

The eighth graders challenged members of the school's faculty to a basketball game in order to raise money to bring down the cost of the eighth-grade trip. I was asked to play, and I know I'm probably the worst basketball player in the city, and much to my amazement I said I would, but there would be one condition.

"Only one?" they asked.

"My class cannot get more than three zeroes for the entire week."

It seemed a simple enough request, and it worked, until the day of the big game. Now you need to know that I don't own a pair of basketball shorts, my gym shoes are tore up and raggedy, and I don't even know if I have a pair of white socks anywhere. So I went out and bought some new gym shoes—twenty-four dollars. I haven't paid that much for shoes in ten or fifteen years. I dug through my drawers and found one pair of sort of white stockings. One of the school volunteers told me he would lend me some basketball shorts. Team shirts would be provided.

The morning of the game, my class had to present their research project. This was six weeks of work. Not one day. Not two weeks. Six weeks. And though most of the students tried, nine students didn't do anything at all. Nine zeroes. Yay! I didn't have to play. And I'd get my twenty-four dollars back cause I didn't really have any need for those new gym shoes.

It didn't happen. Eighth-grade girls came into my classroom after they heard and talked to every one of the students who earned zeroes. OK. I let them in. And it worked. An hour later, all nine of them made a presentation. Not much of a presentation, but a presentation that earned twenty points out of a possible three hundred. Twenty points is no longer a zero.

I had to play.

So here I am, 3:15, in the bathroom changing into basketball shorts so big I have to pull the drawstring with all of my might, pulling up my sort of white stockings (we'll call them off white), putting on my new gym shoes, and the red shirt they gave me.

I walk into the gym, the edges of the basketball shorts tickling my knees (how do you get used to that?) and the students start applauding. Applauding like I'm a superstar. I would smile if I didn't feel so out of place. Everywhere people are warming up. And now they're high fiving me and chanting my name. I try to figure out where I can hide.

After all, I knew I had to be the worst basketball player in the city. Probably in the state.

The game starts and I'm a starter. The ball is passed to me. I take a shot. I miss. Not an air ball. At least it hits the backboard. I pass once, take a pass and pass again. That's enough. With my help the other team is winning. Not by a little either. The score is eleven to four.

I have to tell you I pretend to play in every quarter. At least my son will be proud. "Every quarter? And you weren't tired?" How would I be? I only ran back and forth a few times, the other players quickly knew not to pass to me (one open pass bounced off my knees into an eighth grader's hands and he easily scored), and I couldn't even contain my own students (even though I towered over them).

No matter. It was fun. We lost by six—73-67, but the school raised some money and I humiliated myself in front of everyone.

OK. Here's the deal. No zeroes for the rest of the month and I'll eat an earthworm sandwich. But there's a catch. I'm not letting the eighth-grade girls in to convince everyone to do their work.

—-

The Second Student/Teacher Basketball Game—if you could call it that:

OK. First, here comes Stanley who purchased the shorts for the game—and he gives me extra-large. (I didn't think I was overweight, but I'm starting my diet tomorrow—or probably sometime next week.) I had purchased new shoes for the first teacher/student game. Socks came courtesy of Nike—I guess they heard about my sort of white white socks.

So I changed in my classroom and made my entrance three minutes into the first quarter, my way too large shirt tucked into my way too large shorts. Nothing like walking into a game and not warming up.

(I pulled my t-shirt out a few minutes later. Why didn't any teacher tell me they were supposed to be worn outside of the shorts even when they looked like a dress?)

And I made my grand entrance. Every student lined up against the wall threw out his/her hand and we did that thing you always see with late night hosts—I must have smacked fifty hands before I made it to where my team was seated.

I played for one minute in the first quarter, or rather I should say, I ran up and down the field wide open the entire time for one minute. Good exercise.

Second quarter came and I played for two minutes. Didn't even get close to the ball, but I think—though I'm not sure—that I was able to stay on my man—an eighth grader who was much quicker and better than me. Anyway, he only got one shot off and, of course, it went in.

Third quarter I got a chance to handle the ball. Finally. It went out of bounds and I was the one who passed it back in. Then I was wide open and the students and parents started yelling, "Brownstein's open! Brownstein's open!"—but all I did was run back and forth—and, of course, look good.

Meanwhile the eighth-grade teacher was hot. She was shooting from all angles, hitting the basket sixty percent of the time, racking up the points and the security guy was going "Bam! Bam!" every time he took a shot 'cause he was our star.

We were losing so they let me in for the last five minutes of the game. (They knew to save the best for last.)

Meanwhile the eighth grade teacher grabbed one of her students by the collar and dragged him a few feet across the floor (and she's not even five foot five—but she's strong!) and the security guy began to play punch one of the tall seventh graders when the ref wasn't looking and the seventh grader hit him back (all in play) when the ref was looking so we got a few points through free throw penalties.

I did get the ball again, and I was open and I turned to shoot when this eighteen-foot student jumped all over me before I could even think to raise my arms so I passed it to the eighth grade teacher and she took a shot and made it. I got the ball a second time and this time I did get off a shot which at least hit the rim—but guess what? —I got the rebound and was able to pass it to one of my teammates who at least had a clue.

Great game.

We lost 82-52.

I keep saying this: Basketball's not my game. I'm not sure of baseball. Why can't we have a field hockey game? OK. OK. I'm the only one who can play that. But everyone can run.

Track and field anyone?

8.

Why do teachers fail?

Interesting question. Do they lack the skills to teach, to communicate, to be the constant actor on the stage entertaining for five to six hours? Perhaps they do not have the knowledge to teach what they teach? Perhaps they think teaching is just a paycheck?

I don't know. There are times when my students try me to the point of—well, I don't know. I guess some days teaching school is like getting hit by someone who runs a stop sign and then jumps out of their car hysterical because you were in the way.

I do have an idea though. The community can be a negative influence. So can the parents.

Case in point:

I was put in charge of keeping order during my school's annual field day activity. The local alderman for once helped out and the streets surrounding the school were closed. A corporation came through with a giant enclosed jumping ride. Someone else showed up with a train. The teachers and staff had so many good ideas, every child was busy.

Except for two.

Once again, their teacher had some kind of an emergency and was supposed to show up at 9:30. The teacher aide watching the class could not control these two boys. Two cousins. Both fourth graders. They ran from the room and tore up and down the hallway yelling and whooping it up. I thought they thought they were at a rodeo.

I stopped them. Contained them. Held onto them until I found out their teacher was not going to show. A substitute took the room. No way were these two boys going to be put back in that class.

Just so you know: On any average day, I end up with at least three students from other classrooms because their teacher needs a timeout.

So they remained with me, begging to go on the rides, participate in the carnival activities, and visit the African-American cowboy who was demonstrating his skills in the gym.

Then I saw the bigger one's mother.

"What did they do?" she demanded. She wasn't angry. Really, she wasn't. She was more disappointed.

I told her how they disrupted the school running up and down the halls yelling and screaming.

"What are you going to do with them?" she asked.

"They'll stay with me. Unless you want to watch them."

"Sure," she replied.

"But I need your assistance," I told her.

She asked me what she could do to help. I told her I would rather they did not get to go on the two rides. I thought that was an apt punishment for disrupting the school. She readily agreed.

You know how the story ends. She brought them closer and closer to the best ride. Each time I saw her moving them—past the ring toss, past the three-legged race, past the popcorn machine—I reminded her of the punishment we agreed on.

"Don't worry. I only want them to see what they're missing."

The next time I neared the jumping machine, guess what? Oh, you already did.

You're right. They were in the jumping machine having a blast. And this wasn't their first time either. Her being a parent seemed to get her extra privileges. This was their third time.

She's on the school's Local School Council as a parent representative.

It's no wonder we have problems.

9.

A week to go—and now this:

One day I asked one of my students who curses all the time where he learned to curse so well. He told me one of the teachers cursed all the time and he learned the words from her. It's interesting. He comes from a house of alcoholics and drug addicts. When he would get suspended, his extended family allowed him to go outside every day. One time he got in serious trouble—police trouble—but thirty minutes later there he was playing basketball as if nothing had ever happened.

I spend time every year explaining to my class what true parental love is. I say love is not just feeding you and clothing you and finding a shelter for you. That's an obligation. If your parent can't do these things, there are laws to make them change. I tell them a loving parent knows how to punish their child, how to listen, how to keep them safe, how to make time for them and give them a variety of experiences.

I can't believe a seventh grade boy will hit a girl on the face with the metal handle of a broom and break her skin so badly, she needs stitches. Why did he do this? She was throwing things and hit him by mistake. But she apologized and smiled at him. Not once. Not even twice. She apologized four times. After the fourth apology he hit her on the face. He would have done more damage but she protected her face with her hands when he swung the second time. Did he show remorse? Of course not. Not until his grandmother commanded him to. Did he lie to everyone? Of course. He said he apologized. He said he did not shrug his shoulders as if he didn't care. He said—but what does it matter what he said.

So one of the seventh students decided she had to go to the 8th grade party even though she knew it was only for 8th graders. She threw one of her temper tantrums. Usually her parent will side with her and let her in. Not this time. This time she was not allowed in. Instead she was sent back to class. She never made it. She put her head down on a desk outside and cried the entire time. At the end of the day, she tried to get in again and again her parent sent her out. My student was confused. Temper tantrums always worked before. Why not this time?

Too many times parents create individuals to become future monsters. Unconditional support under every circumstance is not the answer. True parental love includes the ability to set limits, make limits and enforce limits.

10.

When I walked the four miles to school today, everything was perfect. A perfect breeze. A perfect blue sky. Perfect songs from the songbirds in the perfect trees full of perfect blossoms and perfect leaves. The perfect springtime temperature.

School began perfectly too. No trouble on the playground. A great pick-up basketball game. A fantastic game of tag by the slides. Some of the best double Dutch jump roping you ever saw. There was even a contingent of seventh graders discussing trigonometry and their class essay assignments.

Wow.

We started reading stories from character education books, went to writing our reflections of the year, did some silent reading, a fraction review, got to take a brief and very easy twenty minute recess, and then we played around with K'nex to discover the properties of the right triangle.

"More trigonometry?" one of my students asked.

"Not the complicated trig we have been working on. This is simpler," I answered.

"You're joshing us."

Joshing? I haven't heard that word in a long time.

"No," I answered, "you're brilliant. It'll be a no-brainer."

We went into the Pythagorean Theorem and they stayed with me through the entire process. Everyone in the class did all ten problems. Everyone was present today and everyone earned a hundred.

Now there's nine days of school left. I don't know. The way my class is cookin' with grease maybe we should petition the Board of Education to extend everything a few more months.

Did I actually write that?

—-

OPERA OF THE WOOD

The silence of the forest is not the silence of the empty classroom, the teacher bent over

his desk grading papers, a book open to page 202, a soft breeze blowing through a crack

in the window. It is not the city at 3 AM, a residential street, everyone asleep, the cat

leaning into the grass to nap. The forest is the love song of the loons, the call of the

killdeer, the sigh of a breeze passing through the leaves, the first fish surprised by a

development of legs pushing itself out of the water into the tall grass where the crickets

tell the temperature and the grasshoppers play in the leaf. The opera of the trees is just

that grand, the wind that perfect, the harmony of the birds exactly right.

11.

Thursday and here is how the day went—T. had one of her daily temper tantrums ten minutes into the school day and her teacher sent her to me.

A. from across the hall was sent to me because he was acting too silly. I kept him about twenty minutes. Then it was time for his graduation practice so he went back to his room.

Lunchtime and the gym teacher who is a sub was screaming in the hallway because there is no supervision in the gym. He's the gym teacher. Isn't he supervision? So I'm delegated to find out what was going on and what I find is a room full of 8th graders, but they are all in their seats and no one is acting crazy. Well, almost no one. L. and S. were in the gym running back and forth, neither one of them an 8th grader. They leave the gym the second I tell them to and then everything was back to quiet.

My class and I studied the sine of angle A in trigonometry. It's always nice when you see engaged children trying to understand something that is difficult—especially when multiplication and division is already hard. But they are beginning to get it. And learning how to divide at the same time.

OK, so I became the room for the unwanted again, but look at all the great things we accomplished. After all my classes were able to identify literature concepts from Sherlock Holmes, the famous detective we are reading about in language arts. And the research handed in today was top notch.

All in all a very nice day.

12.

I had a READER'S DIGEST moment. You know the kind. You ask who is buried in Grant's tomb and someone yells out, Mark Twain. Or a question on a worksheet wants to know where the survivors will be buried if their plane crashes on the Canadian/American border and a few individuals write Mexico. And you wonder where did these answers come from?

OK. We're studying the development of words and we're looking at the history of the word "Iowa". The question before us is where did Iowa get its name and almost every seventh grader wrote the Iowa River named by French settlers. But then we move on and try to discover how Illinois was named. The choice? Iowa, Sioux or Illinois. Why do more than half the class write down Sioux?

13.

September 1st. I'm back in my classroom. I have to get the class ready for school on Tuesday. I arrived home late, did not get a good sleep, began my walk to school (all of four miles), and got lucky and received a ride from a former teacher. We had meetings in the morning, but I was able to get my room almost ready in the afternoon. What did I do?

cleaned the classroom,
placed tables in their correct place,
put all of the furniture where they are supposed to go,
moved twenty boxes,
created a classroom library by sorting through over four-hundred books,
organized a science library,
organized a science table,
distributed items for primary grades received during the summer.

The day before school starts?

went to meeting at 8:45,
listened to a presentation on standardized tests in reading, math, writing and science,
explained to the faculty about the Least Restricted Environment Project,
presented to the faculty how my classroom did so well in science (we scored in the 90's on the standardized science test),
listened to another presentation,
watched a DVD for inspiration,
sang the song, "We're On the Move",

worked on bulletin boards—five of them in all with a teacher aide,
organized classroom work for Tuesday—first day of school,
wrote letter to parents,
wrote classroom rules, expectations, consequences, homework and school supplies,
created first part of word wall—science vocabulary terms,
set up computers,
received three in-kind grants during the summer and inventoried them,
assisted a former student in getting a poem published,
went through over three hundred pieces of mail—mail from the summer,
worked on some correspondence,
attended a CSMI meeting for science,
wrote out my class list,
wrote my supply list,
checked my Board of Education email,

It was hectic and I was manic.
The assistant principal has just made an all call that the school will be closing at 6:00 sharp. It's almost six now.
Gotta go.

14.

Today is the first day of school and it looks to be a very interesting school year. Due to budget cuts and a drop in enrollment, we lost five teacher aids and two teachers. Nonetheless, we still have a student body that is 98% eligible for the federal free lunch and free breakfast program. Welcome back.

It rained last night and the weatherman informed me it was going to rain in the morning, but the clouds cleared and I walked to school without even encountering a sidewalk puddle. A whole lot of people were in a very good mood this morning—based on all of the hellos I received. (Probably have children going to school!)

I did my final preparations—seating chart, paperwork, etc.—and went to the office for my supplies. I seldom ask for much, but I do like to start the first day of school with pens and pencils for my students, index cards, and at least ten sheets of paper per student. We did not have any writing paper so I had to take a ream of little people paper. (You know the kind—the paper with the big spaces.) There were no index cards, but a teacher gave me sentence strips and I cut them into index card sized pieces. I ended up using Post-Its at each table.

I'm psyched for this new year, almost excited. I even walked the four miles to work in just about an hour. I accomplished everything I needed to do in almost no time.

Anyway—here goes. In fifteen minutes my class will be arriving—and I'm ready for them.

The first day went so smoothly, everything was just about right. Well, there were a few problems. The principal had to give my class gym because the gym teacher hired for the school is on a half-day schedule—he spends one half of the week at another school and the rest of the time with us. The assistant principal taught library. (We still do not have a librarian.) We only have two aids and they seemed to be stretched pretty thin. Only one copier worked. (Out of three.)

I have twenty-four students on my roster, but one transferred out. Twenty students showed up on the first day all in uniform and everyone had some school supplies. (Nonetheless, I still passed out paper, pencils and pens to everyone so those who might not want others to know they could not afford basic supplies were covered.) The class seemed pretty nice and articulate. Two students already told me they had problems with math. Three others asked for help in reading. I'm getting a good feeling about all of this.

Tonight is the first union meeting and since I'm the delegate, I guess I'd better go.

OK—so far so good. We read from a few books, did a pattern in math (using a coloring book), reviewed basic math, studied a chart and graph, and wrote an essay on how to improve the school. We began character education with a story about someone innocent who gets drawn into a police incident. It's good to know my students can tell the difference between a tattletale and doing the right thing. (At least a few students vocalized that view.)

I guess that's it.

The first week of school ended with a smile and a laugh. I have a great class of students! They actually do what I ask and have this need to learn and they're not afraid to ask questions. How cool is that?

On my board, we went over the rules and consequences. We talked about my expectations. We did this every day at least once. Sometimes twice. This class actually responded to them.

"If you have a question, ask. There is no such thing as a stupid question; only stupid people who did not ask."

And they asked. "How do you divide two numbers into four?" "Do you add denominators when you multiply fractions?" "Is there a short cut to this problem?" "I don't see how the boy changed just because he saw an eagle. Can you explain this?" On and on.

Twenty-one students so far—one no show—and two transfer-outs. One of the transfers I knew about. She has too much pride. Last year she refused to do her schoolwork, cursed and instigated, ditched school, was suspended fourteen times and more than once cursed out the principal. One time she got into a physical fistfight with her mother. Her mother!

We had to fail her, but in this school we don't fail seventh graders. My colleague and I worked hard on making her an exception. Her behavior and lack of schoolwork was becoming a part of the culture of the school. We felt the morale of the teachers and students relied on her repeating seventh grade. She bragged she could not fail. No one ever fails seventh grade. We needed desperately to protect the positive culture of the school.

She failed.

She did not believe it. She came to school the second day to get her report card to see if she did, in fact, fail. She found out she was in my room. Fifteen years old in seventh grade. She turned around, told someone she was going to the office to transfer herself out (which we all know she cannot do), and then walked out the back door and hopped on the first Number 3 bus that passed.

She transferred out today. I wish her the best. The streets of Chicago were too open to her and she thirsted for them. No one had any control over her. Not her mother. Not her grandmother. Not us, her teachers. She is going to live in Wisconsin. I hope this works for her. I hope she reconsiders her life and strives to go forward.

The first week of school is over and my class did too many good things. I'm proud of them. I'm beginning to think this will be a great year.

I usually have to go to a student's home the first day or two of school. I'll be honest: I try very hard to get to a student's home the first few days to set the mood for the school year. It's inevitable that someone gets three checks and so off I go walking them home.

This definitely sets the tone.

As a rule kids don't want you walking them home to meet their parent because they are in trouble. Especially not the first day of school. But it does make a very powerful statement. And it works very well, too.

Not this year. I've only been to two houses since school started—two in six weeks. (And they were students from another classroom.) This has to be a record for me. I'm going to begin going for good news starting Monday, but I may go tonight. Haven't really decided yet.

My class and I had some fun with sheep eyeballs yesterday. We discussed the culture around them, how some people pickle them and eat them as snacks and some of the children decided they had pits in them—like olives (I made that suggestion myself)—so it was a bit hard for them to make the leap and see them as a major component of the eyeball.

A few of the girls were scared at first, but then they got into it. (And I have to be truthful again—I had a lot of fun with their fears. Changing the configuration of the classroom, sitting next to them, etc., etc., etc.)

Our mold experiment is going very well, but our protist culture froze in the last few days. It's close to 32 outside and the school's boiler has not kicked in yet. (I had to allow the children to wear their coats inside and I'm wearing mine as I write this.) We'll be looking for life forms in the soil specimen next week.

I'm putting out my dissection specimens today. A whole table dedicated to the materials we will be studying. I have brains and hearts and even half of a goat's head.

This is how I always thought school should be—all of us engaged in learning, me not having to discipline so much, and everyday leaving the school knowing I have benefited from being there.

Thanks.

15.

Desolate,

a growing fire begins in your nose

and somewhere at the back of your neck,

an intangible.

—the first four lines of HOW IT CAME TO BE THIS WAY,

written crossing the great empty lot near the 43rd Street Station, Green Line

And so it begins again.

The boy in the first floor primary room so terrified of walking home by himself, he flinches at the wind, the flutter of a piece of paper, the movement of an adult holding her son's hand. And I am asked to make sure this child gets home safely.

Where is the danger? I need to know this. Why is he so frightened?

He cannot even wait for me. He walks ahead. Stops. Walks a few more feet. Turns at an imaginary sound. Stops.

I am reminded first of the only time I was unlucky enough to see a cat play with a mouse. I can never forget the look in the mouse's eyes. There was something there. A real something. A great fear? A lost soul? This boy has the same look. Only it's not just in his eyes, it's in the movement of his arms, the way his legs drag suddenly, the quick turn of his head as if the drizzle raining on both of us can cause blood to run down his nose.

Then I remember another time. A young girl leaving DuSable High School. She had long blonde hair and the look of someone who belonged anywhere else. It was her first day in that school—and her last. She had chosen to change the fabric of the school integrating it—the first white student.

I can't tell you what started everything off. I don't know why three older girls chased her down the street. All I know is I was walking to the tutoring center after my teaching day ended—this was a few years back (maybe fifteen years or so)—and there she was near the hardware store on 51st, frozen, the three girls getting ready to lunge at her, and she standing too still, her eyes like the mouse, her arms shaking visibly at her side, no expression at all on her face. Just a terrible fear, a terrible horror, a tangible smell. I blocked the girls—and grabbed their victim—but she was not whole. She had no weight. She could not move. I was forced to physically lift her out of harms way and I carried her into the store. She was no longer flesh and bone. She had become a piece of cardboard. I waited with her until the police came and drove her to safety.

Now I am with this child. He must be in third grade. This is my second encounter with him. The security lady tells me every-day other students attack him. Every day she has to walk him home. She can't this day. This day she has another fight to contend with. It becomes my responsibility.

This morning it is still drizzling. No one is out. I cross the great field full of puddles on my way to my school. Everything is colorless. I have already made arrangements for the child to come to my room at the end of the day.

I can still see the eyes of the mouse begging for something. I can still feel the teenager turning to cardboard, her very body corrugated paper, not the flesh and blood of a person. No one deserves to be this frightened.

Desolate

a great fear rising at the hairline,

the useless limbs at the end of the shoulder,

time a patient fool...

16.

I don't understand what has happened. When I went into teaching thirty some years ago, I knew I wasn't going to become the richest man in America. In fact, I knew I was going to spend a lot of my own money, spend hours volunteering, and end up doing a lot of things to assist my students with no hopes of ever being compensated.

Yesterday I asked a few teachers if they would like to do the After School All Stars Program after school for two days a week and two hours a day. I'm the coordinator. I'm rather excited about the entire project. We'll have creative writing classes, dance, drama, and a whole lot more. I'm paying the teachers thirty dollars an hour. Yes, that's correct—thirty dollars an hour.

"I wouldn't work for thirty dollars," one of them told me.

"I never do anything for the Board if it's not my hourly pay," said another.

"After School All Stars. No way," said a third. "No, I'm supposed to get my hourly pay."

I'm sorry.

At what point did teachers decide this was really just a job, the students customers, and the value of teaching a paycheck?

Thirty years ago I knew I'd make a comfortable living as a teacher. I never aspired to be a principal. I went after my masters to become a better teacher. I write grants to make my classroom and school a better place. School starts in an hour. I'll be here past four. I always am.

Somehow the passion of teaching has gone to the wayside.

This may be the biggest problem in teaching today—at least in the large urban inner-city school system I work for.

17.

One year I was the Resource Teacher, a cushiony job. I had extra breaks and sometimes I would be freed up to do other kinds of things. At 2:20 each day, while other teachers were getting their students prepared to go home, I had outside duty. Little me. I'm barely 5'8", maybe an inch more. Many of my students are taller than me, stronger than me, bigger than me. Yet this outside duty was something I actually grew fond of doing.

That was a rough year for my school. No Child Left Behind had turned us into a receiving school and the sending schools sent us the worst children they had. There was almost a fight a day. I got so I could smell conflict before it even started. And that's why I enjoyed it so much. I became THE MAN WHO BREAKS UP FIGHTS. After a while, the students would see me coming toward them and the fight would break up before it began. How easy was that?

So last Friday, on the way to my first home visit of one of my students, I had to jump a chain link fence and stop seven or eight boys from kicking one boy when he was down. Just like old times.

Everyone ran when they saw me. It's nice to have the touch. The downed boy got up and ran towards the school. I followed him with my eyes, saw him reach security—where he remained until the other boys dispersed—and then I went on my way.

The boy is a bully. Some time's we as professionals don't even know if he has the true concept of right and wrong. He had started a food fight in the lunchroom. Could it be he was blaming these boys for his mishap? Could it be he jumped on them as a group thinking his loud abrasive self would be intimidating enough?

I don't know.

People tell me quite often the best cure for a bully is a quick and painful beating.

Was this what this was? Is it ever right?

18.

How My Teeth Came to be This Way and the Choices I Made Because of Them

Have little to do with my wife's obsession with snakes.
She turns off the heat a few hours before bedtime waking me
early with the tired rhythm of cold blood.
Some mornings cold wipes the floor with Saran Wrap and she
remains undercover till noon.
Other times she unhinges herself from bed in a slow stretch of
wills to let in the sun.
There is always enough stored here and there to fix everything
broken, but there is school, a studio for music, a need for a
new boiler, my promise to tuck point this summer.
When she finds her fingers are warm enough to bend, and her
wrists, and her elbows, she bends her long legs and tells me
to add earthquake protection to our long list of bills.
As frightened as she is of snakes, they are always around her—
at the Katie Trail where we walk, in the bushes near the
restaurant where we eat, near the opening of our sub-
basement.
Sometimes late at night, her warm body near, I know her heat
as the grip of a constrictor.
She owns a python's strength and sometimes a rattler's
sadness, and still she loves me regardless of my teeth.
I try not to find myself in tooth loosening moments, but they
find me, one loose tooth at a time.
See this missing tooth? That happened when a gang of
teenagers with one or more guns jumped one of my
students.

He is still alive and for his life, I donated that tooth.
I can explain what happened to the rest, but it is only more of the same.
Have you ever seen someone allergic to cats? Then you know how the cat always welcomes them into its household.
That is the way of snakes and my teeth, my wife and my outrage, how sacrifice really does describe all of us.

19.

Edgar Allan Poe and my classroom:

We just finished reading Edgar Allan Poe's short stories. They're rich in vocabulary and detail. "Morella" really got my class excited. They didn't understand how the coffin could be empty, but then they went through the story again and discovered the baby began to breathe after the mother died, why we need to explore the lives of others, and how insanity moves within us.

The protagonist—if you could call him that—began as a loving husband to a beautiful and accomplished wife, but somewhere in his mind things began to change. She became hideous, her voice nauseating, even her touch cold to his hand. When she died, no longer loved by him, during childbirth, their baby took its first breath after the mother took her last. Suddenly my class made a number of connections. Was the baby Morella come back to life? She looked just like the first Morella, sang like her, had the same need for life. But why did her father keep her isolated?

We delved into the neighborhood of my students.

"We didn't know beating us with a belt was not normal," one of the girls said. "We thought everyone did that to their kids."

I asked how many agreed with her. Every child raised their hands. They all knew someone beaten until they were bleeding or had been beaten themselves.

The turn of events took us back to the child. She lived in isolation—total seclusion. "Why was he doing this?" one of the boys asked.

"Did he want to marry her?" a girl answered with another question. "She wouldn't know it's wrong. How could she? She never had a chance to learn. She might think all girls married their father."

And then we were off—into the lives of my students until one of my students said, "Look at Poe. He married his second cousin when she was just thirteen. Was that normal in that time?"

And we were off again. I just watched, the coach on the sideline, my class coming alive as they explained the demons and fiends that ate at the main character's brain in the story.

When she died, they knew he did not kill her. But why did she die? Revenge, came their answer. The first Morella wanted him to suffer the loss of her love again. And then we were in Greek mythology. Is revenge always correct? Should punishment fit the crime?

Prometheus deserved better from the Gods. He helped the humans, didn't he? To have your liver eaten from your body every day is just too much. But Midas? Yes, he was too greedy for gold and the punishments of Hades—they were designed to fit the crime.

There's nothing better for a teacher than to watch a classroom come alive with the study of a story. And there's nothing better than afterwards to hear a student who is often apathetic and uninvolved say, "That story was too cool."

I thought cool was my word.

Friday we had a few teachers out and it was chaos on the second floor. Another teacher and I had to race between two rooms over and over. The substitutes had no control. I think substitute school needs a section on when to let a battle go in order to win the war.

I have to go on outdoor duty now. Three hundred plus students and me and one security guy. Incredible odds, but we have held down the fort for so long now, when a fight is starting to brew, just walking to it cools everyone off. And yesterday a fight was stopped by one of my students—

"Stop with this he says/she says stuff. You're both beautiful and smart."

Both girls heard the smart and beautiful part.

"And another thing. You know no matter what, you'll be friends in an hour."

Sometimes life is good. No fight. Still good friends.

20.

The first thing you notice about mace is how pungent it is. Then you notice the taste. Finally, the eyes begin to burn. This was the order for me. For Stanley, the order came differently. The mace hit him full in the eyes. He bent over and vomited. Then the pain came and he could not see. The third person only felt its anger in his nose, and he sneezed, coughed a bit, drank a few glasses of water and it was gone.

The taste remained strong in my mouth. Someone asked me what happened to my forehead, and when I touched it, it felt tender, but I do not remember anyone hitting me in my head. I don't even remember when the mace was sprayed. One second I was breathing and the next second my entire mouth felt like it had filled itself with a great ugliness.

This is what happened: I walked the special needs child down the street as I do whenever his parents do not come for him. I don't walk with him. He runs ahead of me, looks back, and keeps walking and then runs and turns around again and then runs. When he makes it to the crossing guard at the corner, I know he's safe. The gang that was attacking him no longer seems to be interested in him anymore. Perhaps it's because I walk him down the street. Perhaps they have just lost interest. I don't know.

When I arrived back to the school, the parents were massing. Not parents to pick up their children. Not even parents who come by to help out. No, these were the parents from Hell—the parents who tell their children to fight, you have to fight, I don't care what anyone says, fight, fight, fight, kick some—, beat some—

They have been out before and I stopped one fight. The next day I just stood with them until everyone left and since they no longer had an audience, they left too. But this after school massing was not going to let go.

One of my students came out and they moved towards her—parents and students. The assistant principal immediately got another member of my school to walk her across the street. She went with him. But the parents did not leave. They cursed. They made noises. They kept a crowd of other children around them. So I stood with them.

The other children did not want to leave. This could be how a horror film starts. Everyone smells blood and they can't wash the smell away, so they stay and wait and wait.

I was able to get most of the students to go home, and I might have succeeded with all of them, but the other family came out from their building and crossed the street like an arrow straight into the parents and adults and students who wanted to fight.

Have you ever knocked on a door to get someone inside to safety and the people inside won't open the door? That's what happened at first. Then the surge of bodies reached to the door, the fighting began, and one by one I pushed individuals into the school—even the grandmother who had brought her children across the street—for what?

I heard her scream to follow me. I heard her scream that they should do as I asked. Another teacher was suddenly in the fray. Grandmother broke loose. I grabbed her and pushed her into the school. Then there was a flash of a child and feet and fists and I saw this girl go down and the adults and the students were on her and the teacher and I—Stanley and others—perhaps another adult or two were in the middle of everything.

Someone shot mace. It filled the fight space like a plague. Stanley went down and the fight pressed into him. It took everything we had to push the fighters back and get Stanley into the school for help. He was blinded, my mouth suddenly tasted ugly and everywhere the smell tainted the air.

But it wasn't over. We got one group into safety, but now the other group was going to the front door. They wanted in. They wanted the fight to spill into the school. So there I was at the front door now, giving orders, keeping everybody out.

The police were already on the scene. Stanley was getting first aide from two teachers. Other teachers were in a classroom calming individuals down. I was everywhere.

The police let me go home an hour later. They had my statement. I don't know what happened after that. One of the officers told me someone was going to jail.

I need to tell you this: The parent who would not let it end is also on the Local School Council.

I've had enough.

On the way home the mace dripped into my eye blinding me temporarily.

After the mace incident the police hauled off one child and one adult—the girl's aunt. When they reached the police station, they were processed and held for about an hour when they were told they were free to go. It seems the witness who saw who sprayed the mace wasn't a good enough witness.

Everything fell back onto the backs of the school. Members from the Board showed up and I was asked to testify. They were meeting to see if they should expel the child who had sprayed the mace.

In the afternoon everything hung on the principal's decision. No one was charged with any crime. No one was expelled. I was called down again for the suspension hearing. The adults started bickering. Their children began to talk louder and louder. The principal suddenly looked around and yelled, "Quiet everyone. We have to get along. Everyone gets five days. I'm done. You can go, Mr. Brownstein."

We were asked if we wanted to press charges against any of the adults. We were told to hang together and the police would arrest the adults and prosecute them. I wanted to prosecute. No one else did.

21.

WHY WE TEACH
Teaching is not for the selfish
or for those who have a jealous streak.
Teachers are not bullies
nor are they anger and flame.

We teach because it is our calling.
We teach because it fills us with song.
We teach because it is our passion
like collecting stamps, listening to music,
a long walk in the park with someone we love.
We teach because it makes us dance,
fills us with joy, makes us whole.
(Have you ever seen a smile on the face of a child?)

Why do we teach?
We teach because we are selfish—
we teach because we must.

To offer the gift of knowledge,
assist someone in finding an opportunity for every possibility,
to show a tree and discover a forest,
to find a butterfly, a rainbow,
a prism of color, a prism to self,
the human experience over and over and over again

and bring it to life
and help it develop
and watch it grow—

this is why I teach.

22.

Friday, the day before our two week vacation, and it's raining outside and though I'm not planning a party, I do have enough games to keep us occupied after we do some school work. I mean this is a school.

And my class complains. Everyone is having a party. (Only three classes are.) Everyone is having a movie day. (We only have two TVs in the entire school, but, yes, two classes have doubled up to watch movies all day and another class is watching HOME ALONE over and over again.) We should have free time. (This is much harder. On and off most classrooms are having bits and pieces of free time. I have planned for free time, too.)

They don't know we will be having a game day after we finish our reading, listening, writing, science and homework for the vacation lessons. (I gave each child from both seventh grade classes a brand new book they can keep forever, but they must do a book report on it due the day we come back. So I guess it's not really a gift cause it has strings attached to it. But it's still sort of nice. Most of my students are thrilled. They really want a book. Parents take note. At this point I also want to add I do not pass out candy at Halloween—I pass out books.)

So what do I do? It's ten-twenty and it's raining outside and the moans and groans are getting louder. I line them up. Now they're excited. Are we going to a movie? Are we going to gym? Nope. I'm taking them to the front of the school so we can read the sign.

Someone please read the sign outside to me.

______ School, one of them says.

Not __________ Party Place? Not _________ Gym? Not ________ Free Time All Day Academy? I ask.

No, they answer, and I think most of them get it, so we go back upstairs.

This is School School. Even on the day before our vacation. Time for the essay lesson. And we do it. And most of my students do it very well, thank you.

23.

The Christmas Carol—A Socratic Discussion:

Monday morning. Reading. We're doing Charles Dickens, THE CHRISTMAS CAROL, and I'm way up for this. I have divided my classes into small five to six people focus groups. We're discussing the segment with the Spirit of Christmas Yet to Come.

And it's great.

"Do they have the right to steal?" I ask.

My students search the text. They spout their own opinions. Yes, they feel, in this case it can be justified.

But does the text justify it? Is there any rationale offered that allows for stealing?

Scrooge is laid out on his bed. He's dead. The three individuals he employs are rifling through his stuff. He's dead. What will he care?

When is stealing OK?

And we go all over the place. One group justifies the stealing because of poverty and greed. Who will get Scrooge's stuff? Why can't it be them?

A second group hears a strong argument for when stealing is OK. If it's on the ground, why can't you just take it? But what if you know who it belongs to?

Doesn't matter. They left it on the ground. It's up for grabs. But isn't your book bag in the closet on the ground? According to you, it's OK for me to take and keep.

And each group goes around and around.

I have to prompt some groups and others I just sit back and listen.

In the end every group concurs: Stealing is wrong. There is no justification for it. It does not matter how evil Scrooge was. It doesn't matter how moral and/or Christian his workers are. All that matters is stealing is wrong.

And then I ask: Is Scrooge responsible for Tiny Tim's death?

And everything begins again.

A great day!

24.

Nine Ways to View a Bully

1.

It is our nature to stop and view the lightning.

2.

Stones, too, can be named

3.

The biggest mouth belongs to a fish.

4.

When you run with garbage, you begin to stink.

5.

Rape is not always a physical act.

6.

The man you think you break may be the one who owns the glue.

7.

Everything will come, my friend, on the wind or in a storm, on feathers or rust.

8.

The best way to view a bully is from a distance and off to the left.

9.

Perhaps all that is needed is a tree.

—-

25.

The Science Fair

Everyday this week I worked on the all school science fair. Monday I judged all of the classroom science fairs (with the help of two hand picked seventh graders). Tuesday and Wednesday students from the fourth to eighth grades came to my room to be judged and/or show me the improvements they made so they could be in the science fair. On those days, my seventh graders assisted every student who wanted to enter.

My room was an explosion of activity. Poster boards laid out everywhere. Staplers coming and going at the speed of sound. Scissors making music you could dance to. It was great. It was exhilarating. It was fantastic. It was—oh, my, oh, my, oh, my—fun! It's what a classroom of learning should look like.

At the end the room was a mess—but my students helped create more than fifty graphs and charts, beautify over forty posters, and practice the presentation with thirty or more unsure students.

This is why I like my class.

(Even if a ton of poster board border littered the floor and the tables.)

Today—Thursday—is the school science fair. Over a hundred students qualified. Over a hundred. How cool is that?

Every evening, every morning, walking through the halls of the school all I hear: Do you have any more poster boards? Can I come to your room for help? How can I make a graph? Etc. Etc. Etc. Please, pick me. Pick me. I have a great project. Pleeeeease!

And the projects are great. The enthusiasm is that grand. The gym is set up and everything is almost ready. I can't wait. In an hour and a half over a hundred students in my school will be set up to be judged and viewed in the largest science fair I have ever run. Hope I get some kind of help.

So here it is, 9:00 and the children are lined up to come inside and I have thirty minutes to go before the science fair begins. We split up my class—they stay outside and have gym with 211—and I go through the final touches.

9:30: Over a hundred projects are on display in the gym and I'm feeling really good about this. One judge does not show, but no problem. The social worker volunteers to take his place and so does a parent volunteer.

One third of the school is in the gym, I'm in charge, the judges are judging—everything is arranged. All I need to do now is walk around and monitor behavior and view all of the projects.

But I made a mistake. There is a seventh grade student who I failed last year and believed beyond reason her pride would not allow her to come back to this school (and I was right until she got kicked out of the school she transferred to in Wisconsin), She is back in the school now—about two weeks—not my room, but I have her for science and reading each day. Last assessment she did the very best in the seventh grade so I did to her what I do to all successful assessors—I placed her name on the classroom website, printed out the page for the outside bulletin board and her mother, and bragged about her.

This is the good part. She started doing well with everything. Including assisting younger children on their science projects. She did, in fact, help one student develop a very nice science poster for the science fair just two days ago.

So what do I do? I reward her. I add her to the list of three students from my class to help me monitor and judge the science fair. (I had created a simple rubric for them to use when they judged the primary grades.) And she is great. An objective, but nurturing judge.

An excellent monitor. She helps set the projects up. She helps build confidence in the little ones.

And then—

Well, then she accuses an eighth grader of spitting on her. This is not true. I am watching when she walks by the eighth grader. But truth doesn't matter when you suddenly have an urge to go off. So I lift her off the ground—and she must weigh as much as me (she's actually bigger than me)—and remove her from the gym through a side door.

I know this girl. So I go to the front door of the gym and stop her from entering through one of the main gym doors. This time I walk her to the office.

She tries to come in a second time and a third and a fourth and a fifth. Each time I have to put her back in the office. How is she getting up and coming to the gym each time is beyond me, but she is. After the fifth time, after I assist her to a seat in the office again, after I shut the door behind me, I go to the cafeteria to reconfirm the lunch schedule. And when I come back into the gym—to the largest science fair I ever compiled—to one of the best I have ever run—there was Big Stanley, one of the judges, pushing two girls out the door.

She has escaped from the office a sixth time and has grabbed the eighth grader who has no choice really but to defend herself. So here I am, next to Big Stanley, pushing the girls out of the gym.

And that's where it should have ended. There is already a police officer in the office. He comes running out to see what the commotion is. And then all of us are knocked together by the rush of students joining the fray.

Suddenly the allies of the seventh grader are in the hall jumping on the eighth grader. This, in turn, brings every family member of the eight grader into the hall.

I have to admit. The police are on it. Suddenly everywhere I look there is an officer. But I am still in the middle of everything. Freeing this girl from this boy. Getting hit on the head eight or ten times forcing another girl from—who knows. Once I even have to move an officer out of the way because he cannot stop two girls tugging each other's hair.

In the end I am hit in the head too many times to count. My back hurts. My hand feels wrong. I actually order the police to move the Hatfield's and McCoy's to two different rooms in two diametrically opposed directions. I go back to the gym. Order everyone to their places. Everyone runs. Everyone is quiet. I ask for the police to round up the students who were in the fight who are still in the gym. They are removed.

In the office two girls are in handcuffs.

"Who started it?" one officer asks me and I point to the seventh grader who promptly begins to curse up a thunderstorm and a tornado and a few hurricanes for extra effect and then she spits in the policeman's face.

Nothing else to talk about. She is on her way to jail. The eighth grader comes back shortly thereafter and takes up her spot in the science fair. And my adrenalin rush fails and I feel every blow to my head and I go to the bathroom and I shut the door and collapse on the floor.

Collapse.

And stay there, my hands on the ground, my head bowed, and I cannot breathe, I cannot think, I cannot do anything at all.

And I stay that way for a long time.

And that's how the science fair ended.

8:25 in the morning and already there are warnings of trouble. This may be hard to believe, but when you work in the inner city long enough, you can smell the potential of the day as you walk from the train to the school. (I'm not sure this works when you drive to work. I don't think the walk is long enough.) When I leave the train—the Green Line at the 43rd Street Station—there is an unmistakable odor of violence already and violence to come.

Today's trouble comes from an unexpected source—a parent walking her first grade son to the lunchroom for breakfast. Two members of one of the fighting factions of girls are in the hallway and I'm escorting them to the gym or the lunchroom, but not upstairs where they want to go—no supervision—when the parent stops us and asks them why they did not acknowledge her. I stop, too.

"Hey, girl," she points to one of the students, "don't you remember? I was right in there fighting too. I was on your side."

I'm wondering why she is bringing this up. Is she looking for glory? Respect? She's grown. She's not a nineteen year old with a six-year-old son. No, she must be in her twenties. I almost ask her why she needs to do this, but one of the girls tells me they'll go to the gym and then the other thanks the adult for her comment and the adult smiles.

Smiles.

A few minutes later the grandmother of one of the fighters and her grown daughter enter the building. (This even after security is told they are not allowed in.) The grandmother comes in cursing and screaming and rushes towards the office where the principal is standing. Next thing you know she is pushing the principal hard out of the way.

The police are called. They arrive in ninety seconds. Three policemen in full body armor.

How does everything end? It hasn't yet. The grown daughter removes all of her children from the school and I make sure the others are safe and supervised in the school's lunchroom. All of the fighters but two—they were actually victims of Friday's assault—are suspended for five to ten days, the Chicago police will have an officer stationed in front of the school before and after, and Security and Safety have been unofficially notified. We're filling out assault incident reports and the Professional Problems Committee—which I am the chair of—is going to meet on Thursday.

26.

Friday afternoon the office buzzed my room. We're sending an aide to you so you can take an important phone call.

Only emergency phone calls are this urgent. I rush to the phone. It's the teacher's union. They can't read my writing. It's a problem of a change of address. I'm immediately relieved.

But as soon as I hang up the phone, it rings. So I answer it. It's the security guard. Why's he calling the school? He's in the school.

And he tells me. The fight from yesterday happened again at 8:30 in the morning. He got hit in the head this time. He had enough. He's not in the school. He went home. He wants to quit. A bunch of girls who don't even go to the school invaded the front office and the fight that began after the science fair began again.

Nine police cars. One security guard, the assistant principal—a woman, by the way—and a former woman teacher tried to break it up. Thankfully the police were there within seconds. It was as if they were waiting. A lot of people were handcuffed and sent to jail.

The security guard wants to transfer to another school. I end the phone call by convincing him to give the school one more chance. One more chance.

One more chance.

Do you know how it feels to want to cry? This is what I'm thinking as I say it over and over.

One more chance. One more chance.

He said OK and then I went back upstairs to work—my class full of my students, three students from next door and two boys who wanted to fight on the first floor. I don't even get a chance to sit down. A sub is in the hall yelling my name. Yelling it. OK—this is how it continues.

OK—I went to the doctor yesterday. Remember the blow to the head on Thursday last week during the best science fair I ever ran? The day I collapsed. The day I thought—

He listened, examined and then ordered x rays of my neck and a cat scan of my head and told me not to go to school for the next two days.

Did I listen?

I didn't listen the first time when my doctor told me on Thursday to go to the emergency room. Why should I listen to him on Wednesday?

So, yes, I'm here at school.

And what happened yesterday? Confusion down the hall and a room out of control.

CAN WE COME TO YOUR ROOM? Please. Please. Please.

And I would have taken them, too, but I had a doctor's appointment.

Today: We are meeting before school on the security and safety issues since the big fights began. I, of course, am the chairperson for the Professional Problems Committee and I had to call for a meeting. I mean how is it to come to school and there is a police car in front and then go home and there is a police car in front and when you walk down the halls during the school day, women teachers are so scared they lock their classroom doors.

Did I tell you about the man who made an obscene gesture at one of the youngest teachers on our staff? No. Well, now you know. How did he get in? How did he get past the office?

I received a subpoena. The man knocked on my door, no one was home, and he left it at the mailbox. The next day he called my school and I called him back.

Did I receive the subpoena? he wondered.

Of course, I did. One of the students in my school spit in a police officer's face after causing a major fight in the hallway during the science fair. Between her cursing and carrying on, between her throwing things at people when she has one of her frequent temper tantrums, between her walking out of everyone's classroom—and lets not forget the day she cursed out the principal in front of the entire seventh grade class—between all of this, you know I'll be there in court.

But I do have a few problems with all of this. The research I have done on failure with male students of color has shown negative police contact is one of the greatest indicators to future incarceration. Our juvenile facilities do not seem to send reformed individuals back into society. Instead we receive students who are even angrier.

I'll never forget the time I went to visit an acquaintance of mine who was sentenced to a few months in Cook County jail for drunk driving. He asked if I could come visit him and so I went, one cold Saturday, and much to my surprise, too many people knew me. And I'm not talking about the guards.

On the walk to the entrance I met a few families going to visit former students. In the waiting room, I waved hello to a dozen more former students. On the way out, I ran into a family who remembered me as their son's teacher.

Teaching in the inner city is not always the easiest. It's hard to know where to draw the line. It's hard to know when to become the parent because the real parent is not parenting. It's hard period.

So when a student throws an encyclopedia and hits another student in the eye because, well, because the other students accidentally hit him with his notebook—and apologized…

So when a student stands off a group of angry girls with a scissor, and yes, I ask for the weapon and then I escort her home….

So when a thirteen year old starts having sex and then the man—it's hardly ever anyone her own age—dumps her and she begins going into regular cursing depressions and she wants to fight everyone no matter what and hurt people and kick them when they are on the ground…

Where do we draw the line? At what point do we have to decide the parent won't handle it, but the police will?

Today the principal is observing me. This is part of her job description. I'm ready, of course. Then again, I'm not.

There comes a time, I guess, where you have to decide if you are making a difference anymore or if you are just spinning your wheels in a snow storm and your car gets even more stuck.

I had to go to court yesterday. Not really all that bad. I brought enough personal business for three to four hours. Didn't even have to take a sick or personal day. Court—school business.

The girl went for the plea bargain—a year's supervision, anger management, conflict resolution classes, mandatory school attendance, community service.

OK. Mandatory school attendance. This on a girl who ditches school, fights, curses, SPITS IN A COPS FACE, hits another girl in the jaw when she's being restrained by another cop, etc. etc. etc.

But I was back at my desk in two hours.

So today we passed out report cards. Another interesting moment. Children all over glad to get a C.

In my household an A is absolutely excellent, B is beautiful, C means confused, D is a dummy and an F—a failing fool.

I'm confused myself. Court cases. Children happy to get C's. (One-seventh grader was so jubilant, he hugged me.) Parents waiting at the door for conferences.

Oh, and by the way, the court girl was in school today—doing her work. Quietly. All daylong.

She's really quite bright, you know, so we're not giving up on her. But how do you stop someone from giving up on them self?

—

A Death to a Student

They hire a guest preacher to mourn him
And he cannot remember the name.
The oldest son no longer controls control
And the child's teachers sit like snow
Melting quickly into puddles of incoherence,
Black ice, a winter's sorrow.

Outside,
A cruel blue sky, brilliant and malicious sunlight,
Just a touch of gentle cursed wind,
Air so light, it could not lift a weight in tears.

27.

Some days should be a snow day. Six to twelve inches of snow fell over Chicago, heavy snow with thunder and lightning, sleet and slush. In my neighborhood, the emergency alarms went off and even at 5:30AM, when I left to catch my train, sirens of ambulances and fire trucks were flashing down the streets.

When I arrived at school, the snow blower was broken. A few minutes later, there we were, lifting the heaviest snow I shoveled in years to make two paths around the school. Two of us hand shoveling while the third worker tried to figure out what was wrong with the snow blower.

Inside, a bit later, still no one was in the main office—I was in that room for a bit taking phone calls (but none came) until one of our tutors came in and took over.

8:15, the lunchroom opened for breakfast and two people were trying to manage the cafeteria and hallways by themselves. I joined them, going from section to section, line to line. (Did I tell you I already cleaned up the entire LRE room this same morning?)

No fights. No real confusion. No teachers yet, but more adults helping to organize the students. One security officer—my school has two full-time—passed out pages to color. The tutor had decided to consolidate the lines and placed the intermediate students with the older primary children. A lot of students were in the gym watching basketball practice. It was just too bad outside for anyone to be in the playground.

School began at 9:00. Five teachers were not present—three on the first floor and two on the second. Two classes were split up—the special needs class and a small class size third grade.

Outside at dismissal, the snow some of the best snowball snow I have seen in a long time, but very few snowballs flew. Five minutes after dismissal—the sun bright, the air frigid—just about everyone was gone.

So I went home.

28.

Taking Back a Classroom

(Rap talk)

Rough neck,
Rough neck

(Students drum on their desk)

Rough neck.
Rough neck.

(begin singing)

To the neck, to the neck,
Proactive packed in a box
To the neck, to the neck,
Get out the cream
And don't you scream.
To the neck, to the neck.

This is the song a few of the boys in my class made up about one of my students. My classroom is my family. I've taught for over thirty-five years and no one has stolen anything of value from me. (Books from the school library and pencils, pens and paper don't count.) One year when a Chicago team won a championship, people from the neighborhood broke into the school and destroyed almost every room—except for the computer lab and mine. No one has ever insulted me to the point of quitting (though they have come close). I never realized until I began teaching in the inner city how important it is to immediately stop negative talk about someone's mother. (These are serious fighting words.) I've seen serious bullying, extreme violence, and quite a few other things during my time as a teacher. (Once I had to go into a bathroom where a student was holding four other students at knifepoint to talk him out of hurting anyone. When he came back from his suspension, he was placed in my class.)

I'm nearing the end of my career as a teacher. I always thought I might make a difference. I always thought my students were like family. This class this year is one of my best. They're bright, witty, charming, and each one of them contributes something great to the whole. Yet now I have to change my rules and become more explicit. No talking also means no cursing. I have to put on the rule board we cannot bully. I have to add sentences to my expectations. I have to let them know field trips will be cancelled for cursing and bullying incidents. And now the girl in my class who handed me the above song written by a few of my students is bullied to the point of tears. And the boys find this funny.

Fortunately, a few girls are proactive—not the same as the Proactive cream in the above song which is, unfortunately a strong medicine—and they are working to put a stop to this confusion.

I promise you it will stop today.

I always keep my promises.

29.

Roller-skating and physics. They go together like peanut butter and bananas. Like hot dogs and grilled onions.

I put the skates on after lunch. Huh, what's going on? What's Mr. Brownstein up to now? What's he doin'? Mr. Brownstein, the mad scientist. The buzz alone was worthwhile by itself. Why the skates? my students asked.

Physics, I answered.

And we had a physics lesson and I had a workout.

How do you show the laws of motion? Skate quickly to the door, have someone open it before you run into it—and this wasn't planned—keep right on going into the hallway and across the hall and into the door opposite my room that was, thankfully, closed. (An object will continue on a straight line until it hits an obstacle.)

By the way, did I explain I don't know how to stop in these things—brakes or not?

So I taught gravity (falling) and by showing the weight of gravity in a contest between me and a few of my students. (We lifted our legs up—I still had on these heavy, heavy, heavy skates—and we watched to see who would drop their legs first due to the weight of gravity. They won, but I let them, I think.)

Potential energy and kinetic energy? A snap when you're skating around the room. I firmly believe every one of my students can tell you what those two terms mean after my demonstration of an object at rest (me standing still on skates) and an object in motion (me moving on skates).

Of course, we had a chance to study friction, too. No problem. My students worked cooperatively to teach me how to use the brakes. And I got it. I still can't stop on a dime. I probably can't stop on a silver dollar or ten one dollar bills lined up ten long, but I did learn to stop.

OK—I get to do this lesson again with my other science class this afternoon. Can't wait.

30.

The Superintendent of the Chicago Schools is coming to my school sometime during the week of the President's Day Holiday.

So, of course, we suddenly have to make the school perfect and everyone in the world knows no school anywhere is perfect. We are not going to be teachers; we are going to be actors.

Principals, please listen: A school is a school. Almost every teacher I know is passionate about teaching and they are trying as hard as they can.

If the superintendent is coming because he wants to close our school down, no matter how good we look, he will see only reasons to close us down. If he is coming because he is proud of us, no matter how bad we look, he will see only the good.

Once in my life—back in the day when Chicago schools went on strike every year—I ran a school for neighborhood students during the strikes. One teacher, a friend of mine, could not control his students in his classroom and he could not control them in the school I created temporarily. Nonetheless, when the Chicago Tribune showed up to write an article about us, I did not take over his spot teaching the high school students algebra. They were loud, everyone talking, he was at the board chalk on his suit and face, paper all over the table and chairs—not a perfect situation. The Tribune reporter came in with her photographer only minutes after I had let out the elementary school classroom. The place was a mess.

The next day on page 3 of the metro section there was a great and very positive article written about us covering half the page. Instead of noisy students, the reporter used the words "overzealous learners". Throughout the article were the words "engaged," "exciting," "wonderful." Even the mess became a compliment: "a real learning environment."

The photo was great too.

Principals, you don't have to put on an act. Your teachers care about the school, too. Let them do their job. The visitors come to the school with a ready-made agenda. No matter how we do, they will make the situation fit that agenda. Sorry, but that's the truth.

We're teachers teaching in sometimes very terrible and demanding

conditions. We're not actors who put on a show for one day. We're teachers who teach everyday.

Enough said.

—-

Journeys and Journeymen

My mother did not make the trek across earth mountains and rocky beaches.
She allowed us to sail into ourselves one accident at a time.
Nowhere does the graffiti list off every Siberian possibility.
My mother was sweet oil and hard tack, always in full color.
Years go by and time stops.
We knew better and we did not know better.
My mother drove a car into a deer on a country road.
We settled into a denial of one anthropology over another.
A flowering tree has an incredible need to flower.
My mother dreamt us up one brick at a time.

[Mendeleev's] mother must have recognized his precocious intelligence, and when he reached fourteen, feeling that he would be lost without a proper education, she walked thousands of miles from Siberia with him—first to the University of Moscow (from which, as a Siberian, he was barred) and then to St. Petersburg, where he got a grant to train as a teacher. (She herself, apparently, nearing sixty at the time, died of exhaustion...)

Oliver Sachs, Uncle Tungsten

31.

During science today, everyone in both of my classes—well, not everyone (one students earned an 80%)—earned a hundred percent on their anatomy science quiz. I gave a bonus question and one of the boys—one of the biggest discipline problems in the school—knew the answer and wrote it down so well, I just had to let him tell the class the answer.

Then I said, Make sure you thank him when you use his answer.

I didn't know this boy could smile.

First, a girl who has wanted to fight him for a number of days now, pushed him rudely as she entered the classroom and he said, Excuse me, and he went to his seat and ignored her.

Then he went into the computer lab for our poetry project and found numerous commentaries on the poem he is doing for his poetry study.

In the classroom, he handed in his first finished essay of the entire school year.

I already told you about his bonus answer excellence.

So I bragged about him to the class and to his homeroom teacher and do you know what he did?

On the way to art class, he saw a student giving a teacher a hard time. He stepped out of line and said, "I've been there. Let me help you out." AND THEN HE HELPED OUT. He took the screaming student back to the correct classroom.

And that's how my day went. One good thing after another.

How cool is that?

—-

We're reading LOVE THAT DOG as part of our poetry unit. It went well—even the reading of complicated poems later on. Today we're going to add a technology section to the poetry—if I can get into the computer lab. (It stays locked.)

In the afternoon we studied the heart of a cow and the tail of a sheep. A very smelly unit. I purchased both the cow heart and the sheep tail at my neighborhood grocery store for a grand total of $2.14. Together we opened up the heart and the tail and made a study of what we saw.

After the oohs and ahhs and the screams from the squeamish boys and one squeamish girl, everything went really well.

Do people actually eat this stuff? (Yes.) Is our heart really this dark? You're right, (gosh, a teacher being right!) There's a lot of blood on this thing. (It's a heart.) Check out the fat on this thing. Is this cholesterol?

What stinks? This tail is really gross. (This from three boys.) Why does it feel so slimy?

Where is the wool? Why is it so thick? Check out this bone. It this cartilage?

Seventy degrees outside in Chicago in March—a sunshiny day—and we enjoyed ourselves.

32.

You rush the scene and hold the same girl back from yesterday. You try to calm her. She is a curse word, suddenly, not even human anymore. Just a curse word like a wild river spewing from her mouth. You don't know how it began and you don't care. Not this moment.

You rush up to the mother when the other girl is restrained and tell her, Please, take her pregnant daughter into the school.

No, the mother yells at you. We're going to finish this. She practically pushes her daughter onto the sidewalk.

There's nothing else you can think to do but help to restrain the other girl—big and strong, but all of the time you're thinking, Your daughter's pregnant and skinny and sickly, too. If she fights, she will lose and she will lose badly. If you wanted her to have an abortion, why didn't you just set it up in the clinic? Why would you want her to lose the baby right here, right now, on the street?

When calm is restored, it comes out. The pregnant girl—a student who does not even go to the school (with coaxing from her mother)—and her friend—came to start this fight. No motive. Nothing.

So you ask yourself again: If you wanted your fifteen-year-old daughter to have an abortion, why didn't you just do it the right way? Was it an issue of money? Was it a moral dilemma that this fight would resolve?

Why would any grown mother send her pregnant daughter out into a fight she knows her daughter cannot possibly win?

And when do fighters ever really win?

33.

We're at my college class for teachers seeking a science endorsement and here comes one of the teachers.

"What a day. I suspended eight kids from my class." He takes his seat and looks around the room. "Two girls wanted to fight. They're the hardest to break up. You can't just grab them anywhere."

He pauses.

"My school is just a lawsuit getting ready to happen," he continues to no one in particular though all of us are listening.

He pauses again.

"At least the boys are easier. You have at least three minutes lead time before you have to get between them. They got to bump chests and get into each other's face. Girls? Now that's another story."

It's spring in Chicago and it's raining and it's cold. Outside it already looks like dusk.

"My mother teaches in the inner city of Philadelphia. She called me last night to tell me yesterday was the worst day of teaching in her career. It's not getting better."

Then class starts and he doesn't speak for a long time. When he does, it's a question about stem cells. After that he opens up a bit more, but you can tell the melancholy of the day—of his second year as a teacher—weighs itself down on him heavier than stone.

—-

A Visit to the Zoo

I nurture the wrong people,
gangrene girls with color scars,
small breasts like the yellow cusps of dandelion.

I have broken so many fights
the count is beyond fingers,
beyond toes.

We walk the stone paths of the zookery.
Ivy, oat, barley. Great frogs, green shade,
wood ducks, a rock ledge.
Water lilies like thick fish, spotted fish,
striped fish turning delicate hoops.

We eat lunch on stone benches jutting out over water,
a breeze ghosting through spiked grass.

Swifts move through the air like Chinese fighting kites
and there by the fallen tree, an egret,
wings stronger than hunger,
wings stronger than selfishness.
My girls do not see the wood duck, the swift.
They do not see the fish, the large frog.
My girls complain about the walking,
this was a trip to the zoo,
we came to see animals

not Lake Michigan,
not the break wall,

not a rumble of rock blocking waves,
the water green gray blue,
not shells, not algae,
not sand thick with alewives.

I nurture caged girls,
meat-eating girls,
and when the rock dove lands by thrown bread,
I nurture girls who glory in the herring gull's attack,
a rock dove retreating quickly,
wild wings sparking like fields of lasers.

34.

The day after spring vacation and there was a bit of the old confusion, but my class was kick butt strong.

During science my seventh graders and I began to explore the standard deviation equation and they were on top of it. I gave them a number of repetitions, we worked out each variable, they worked by themselves and together cooperatively, and a lesson I thought would be troublesome and last for more than an hour took us thirty minutes and almost everyone had it down.

The best part: two students who are afraid to participate because they did not want others to think they are slow gave me the right answers aloud over and over—and I didn't even have to call on them.

They volunteered it.

OK. OK. I didn't do the entire equation. I dissected it and taught the students variable by variable. When they had this down, I introduced them to the concepts inside of the square root sign.

They understood data, mean, and the summation of the problem. Wednesday we go for broke.

Today I teach the other class the same subject and I'm rip roaring ready to go.

And did I tell you there were no problems whatsoever outside on duty before school and after. Only one student was sent to my room

for discipline and he was fine. Everything smooth sailing and easygoing times.

35.

I came to work Tuesday only to find out the winner of the Seymour Brownstein Most Improved Student Award in honor of my father would not be participating in the graduation. His standardized test scores and report card grades were not good enough. He'd have to go to summer school and then move on to high school. Nonetheless, he was at school to support his classmates. An altogether brave young man.

A few others would also not be graduating including one student whose brother was shot in the face a few days ago murdered only a block away from the school. He did not come to school to support his classmates—and he had a very good reason not to. Life is hard too many times in the neighborhood where I teach.

I did have a runner up ready to take my winners place. When the time came for me to speak, the office called me downstairs, had me place my classroom of students next door or in the art room, and I took my place on the extremely hot stage.

Here's how it went:

The MC stood up after the eighth graders finished singing one of their songs and introduced me: "We are honored to introduce to you one of our seventh grade teachers who has a very special award."

How special? When the principal found out how much money I was giving the most improved student, she said that's more than we're giving our valedictorian. And I said, "Well, that's how it is."

Then the MC said my name and a very nice thing happened. The audience went wild with clapping and cheers and I, of course, felt really good about everything.

"There are two perfect young ladies," I began, "in the class I taught last year and I just want to say they were the best seventh graders I have ever taught. These two young ladies, if I decided to have any more children, I would want two daughters exactly like them." And the audience let out a loud sigh—just like the kind you hear on talk shows when everything is finally perfect. "My father who passed away years ago always honored people who tried. He gave them one chance or two—sometimes even fifteen. All of us are worth that many chances and more. He taught me this. Anyway I chose these two girls because perfect as they were, they became even more perfect in eighth grade."

Then I called them to the stage by name and they came and took their checks and we shook hands and we took a photo.

Then I said, "It was very hard to pick a winner this year. We had a follower who has now begun to show leadership qualities and we had a student I wanted to pick but things went wrong. To him, when you have a lemon, turn it into lots of lemonade and when summer school is over your check will be waiting for you. The winner of the Seymour Brownstein Most Improved Student Award goes to a young man I taught after he was sent to my room last year in the middle of the year. He was well behaved and he did all of his work and he made major changes, but he could not allow negative peer pressure to be ignored. So he began to move in negative directions more and more. Well, this year he has not had a single fight, but he has broken up fights with words and conflict resolution. He has not been sent to the office once for a negative incident." And I heard "amen's" all around me. "He has grown and become a leader and I hold in my hand not one check, but two."

When I called his name everyone on the stage stood and gave him a standing ovation and he was so happy, he hugged everyone, told me, "Thank you, Mr. Brownstein," and beamed through more than one photograph. Then he took the two envelopes—each holding a check for thirty-five dollars for a total of seventy—and proudly went back to his seat.

When I left the stage a few minutes later, I remembered my father and how he always tried to do the right thing and how he always put into us the conviction and strength necessary to help to make this world a better place. So I paused on the stairs for a moment and thanked him.

Then I collected my students and went back to my classroom where my class and I cleaned up—it being the last full day of school and all.

—-

Exploring a Flower

...(T)he beginning of poetry in English occurred when an illiterate farmhand was aroused from sleep by an angel who then prodded him to versify the Book of Genesis.

Robert B. Shaw, "The Muse at Loose Ends"

I who cannot write, write.
There are those who know miracles cannot be miracles.
Thin lipped, her eyes wide open, she stands to sleep
and I wonder if, when night lives, this is her time.
I know the Bible.
I have heard it often enough.
Yet word for word, verse for verse, I cannot read.
Read I must.
She holds the railing,
sways with the movement of this thing she rides,
lips so thin when hair drips before her ears,
they bleed into her face.
I need to meet her.
She can teach me all things.

36.

AND THEN IT BEGINS AGAIN: A NEW TEACHER'S IN TOWN—

My No-BS Guide To Success As A New, Urban Teacher

by Laura Meili

Remember why you wanted to teach at the very beginning. Protect and shelter that naive, hopeful optimist with your life. It will be very difficult to sustain yourself as a teacher without keeping this part of yourself intact.

Read or, better yet, listen to the poem "Teachers" by Taylor Mali. (It can help with remembering the power inherent in our jobs.)

In my first (and every subsequent) interview, I told them I was "tougher than I look." It got me the job, but only because I WAS tougher than I looked!

On the first day of school, your class list looks NOTHING like what it will on the 5th or the 10th. Be ready for TONS of transfers in and out in the first month, and all year!

You can smile in September! But make sure it's at something that's actually funny or happy – not just for the sake of being overly cheerful. Even though it's sad to say, blind happiness could be exploited by students.

Go into your year knowing it will be crazy. If you go in expecting that you're fully equipped to take on every challenge, you're going to have an identity crisis when you realize you had no idea that some of this was even possible. Don't set yourself up to realize you don't have it all. Go in with this humble understanding.

Don't EVER cry! –also known as - keep your weaknesses in check. They need to know you have faith and confidence in yourself and your ability to succeed with them. If you don't have this faith, there's NO WAY they will.

The advice to keep yourself and your personal life out of the classroom is crap. Your kids need to know who you are; this will make them want you to get to know them.

Like Brownstein says, you can't work from 8:30-2:45 and be a successful teacher.

Routines must be there – they counteract all your annoyances. Think of everything that could bug you in the classroom (mine are pencil sharpening, repeating directions, and broken crayons) – most can be solved with some sort of procedure (i.e. no electric sharpener in the room, always write directions on the board/chart, and a NO CRAYON ZONE.)

If you're wrong, GO BACK! APOLOGIZE! Kids need to know that this is how the real world works. We mess up! And then we apologize and go from there...

Jump on the first missteps your students make! DON'T IGNORE behavior at the beginning of the year, or you will have to ignore it all year long. For example, my first year, I ignored cursing and ended up having to listen to it all year. My second year, the first swearword I heard, I mocked a heart attack and made it clear that it was unacceptable for that point forward. Is it perfect? No. But is it better than the first time around? Definitely!

Use HUMOR!!!! It's the most common classroom management technique in my middle school classroom. It has diffused more issues than every other measure combined.

Respecting your kids should always be your first measure of discipline. From there, figure out what works for you/them! They are crazy and you're going to need to be creative. Don't forget this or blame them for acting crazy – it's normal for their age!

Read to kids daily. Write with kids. Race your kids in math to foster competition.

Build in opportunities for students to talk to each other. They'll talk no matter what, so building in this times gives them the chance to talk AND follow the rules!

Don't only ask "how are you" when a kid is looking down. Ask kids how they're doing when they seem happy so you have the chance to talk about something positive!

The second you get yourself into an argument with a student, you've already lost. They are KIDS. Don't forget this and start holding grudges like they're grown.

NO KIDS are too difficult if they have a strong teacher.

When things are going wrong in your classroom, take ownership. If you blame the kids/parents/administration/etc., you'll always have an excuse not to improve.

If you see resources that work in other schools and automatically think "well, that won't work with my students", your students automatically miss out.

Bored kids cause problems. OVERSCHEDULE.

Kids who think an assignment is out of their reach will find any excuse to avoid it.

Teach kids things that matter to them. Teach kids things that matter to you. Your passion will be contagious.

Use creative maladjustment. Find ways to work within a crazy/ illogical system by closing your door and doing what works.

Avoid the "language of consent." Making excuses doesn't help kids read, or do math, or get into college.

Relax. Kids don't like to be around tightly-wound people. Neither do adults, for that matter.

If you have consistent complaints about your kids and their situations and their communities, don't work in these communities! These kids need teachers who are committed to them no matter what they're coming in with. If you can't give them this, get out and save them the disservice.

You can say "it starts at home" until you're blue in the face, but regardless of where it starts, it ends in your classroom. These kids are still your job. Get over home life as an excuse, and improve the way you meet your students where they are.

Silently waiting and staring down is ALWAYS more effective than yelling at the kids. As soon as you yell once, you'll need to yell every time again to prove to them that you're mad. Yelling barely ever works immediately, and neither does quietly waiting, but I'd definitely rather spend my time quietly waiting than stressing myself completely out by yelling like a maniac.

Expect the craziest behavior possible everyday from students and you'll regularly be pleasantly surprised instead of consistently disappointed by them..

Kids need to know that you know they can do it. Just telling them that they can improve their own intelligence makes them work harder! Create a self-fulfilling prophecy that's positive!

Sanity is key! Take time off. When planes are in an emergency situation, they tell you to secure your own gas mask before you help others. You need to take care of yourself first before you can help your kids.

You won't be perfect. Get over it.

—

And so I can retire—now that the new teacher's in town.

www.ingramcontent.com/pod-product-compliance
Lightning Source LLC
Chambersburg PA
CBHW050020170726
48282CB00025B/485